BRANDYLANE PUBLISHERS • P. O. Box 43 • Lively, Virginia 22507

Jane Stouffer Williams

1995

SUPER DUCK

A TRUE STORY

BY

JANE STOUFFER WILLIAMS

FOR CHILDREN OF ALL AGES 2 - 92 WHO LOVE DUCKS!

To

Lewis Shelton, Menhaden Ship
Captain, who gave us our first
ducklings;

the memory of Dr. Ross
Brumback, who taught us how to
raise ducks;

my friend and neighbor, Carol
Hall, who helped edit and type
Super Duck's story;

my wonderful husband, Don
Williams. Together we raised
Super Duck.

Without Don's love and
encouragement this book would
never have been written.

Let me introduce myself -- I'm Super Duck, a wild mallard duck. That's not a name I would have chosen for myself. Don and Jane gave it to me. Maybe I am sort of special after all.

My mother Dewy and father Louie live on a river off the Chesapeake Bay in Virginia. My mother attempted a nest last year in the boathouse that belongs to Don and Jane. Otters ate some eggs and raccoons ate some and, worst of all, the rest of the eggs dried up. My mother really didn't know a lot about brooding and incubating and left her nest to be with my father for long periods of time. She was young and inexperienced in raising a family.

This year Don and Jane gave her more protection from the otters and raccoons by putting obstacles around the boathouse so that my mother had to weave her way into the nest. She used the leaves and pine needles Don and Jane had left for her. Even with all the extra care it was her third nesting attempt this year.

At first her eggs were scattered. She would lay one egg each morning and cover it carefully with leaves. After she had seven or eight eggs she began moving all the eggs together with her bill. Plucking down feathers from her lower breast, she lined the nest and made a cup-shapped depression. But -- she still wasn't ready to settle in for the incubation period until she had laid three more eggs.

Mallard eggs range from white, pale pink, to pale green. My egg and my brothers' and sisters' eggs were beautiful soft green.

Finally satisfied that she had enough eggs and that they were lined next to one another, my mother gently lowered herself, covering all the eggs. After a few adjustments of body weight on July 12th she began her 28-day vigil and my life started.

This year she was a good brooder and only left the nest once a day. Before she would leave, she plucked more down from her chest to cover the eggs and with her bill pulled leaves from around the edges into the nest. There was an old shredded rope hanging nearby which she sometimes tugged on to get soft strands to help cover our nest.

After stretching her legs, which must have been very cramped from sitting so long, she looked in every direction with her head up high to make sure no one was watching her leave her nest. Finally satisfied, she flew out of the boathouse into the water with a loud "Qu-a-a-a-ck!" -- demanding the attention of my father, who was usually nearby.

They had a joyful reunion and splashed a bit in the water, but my mother was hungry and anxious to get back to her nest. They swam to the beach and walked up the hill where Don and Jane had a pan of whole corn waiting and a tub of fresh water. It was hot in July and all the mallard ducks Don and Jane fed enjoyed drinking the cool, fresh water and taking a bath.

Some had their young ducklings with them and were sleeping in the shade of the holly, azaleas and ivy.

My mother knew what she wanted and after filling her crop with corn, forced several small ducklings out of the water tub. She enjoyed dunking her head and throwing water all over her back with her bill and wings. Louie, my father, was right by her side.

It wasn't long before she realized she had better attend to her eggs, and along with my father, waddled down the hill. Then, she flew up on the dock. Cautiously, she peered into the boathouse and slowly moved toward her nest. When she was satisfied nothing was disturbed, she waddled quickly onto the nest.

The brooding pause was over. With her bill on the outside of each egg she rolled us over. Turning all of us several times a day as we developed helped to keep us from sticking to the edges of our shells.

We had cooled down some while she was gone and this too was important in our development. Our eggs had to cool so the air in the egg cavity could contract and fresh air would be sucked in through the pores of our egg shells.

With her wet body she slowly lowered herself over us and moistened all our eggs. This year my mother knew just what to do to hatch our family.

Every day she repeated this process. She gave little soft klucking sounds of love to me as she moved my egg and settled down to warm me. I was growing and filling my egg completely. My mother's faint contact calls to me and my brothers and sisters grew more and more frequent.

I began to peep back -- "Hello, Mother, -- I'm here -- it's me!" Then she would turn me over with her bill.

A lot of commotion started when my brothers and sisters started to hatch. Mother would shift her body and softly kluck to give us encouragement.

I was anxious to hatch and with my egg tooth at the end of my bill began to make cracks -- and then a small hole. I was breathing fresh air! In my excitement I kicked and rolled my egg right out of the nest!

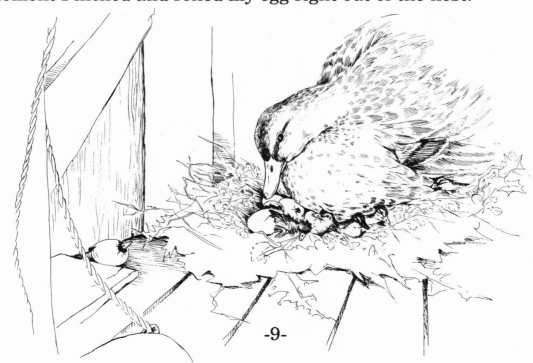

My mother was very busy with the other eggs and didn't see me. I peeped and peeped, rested awhile and began to peep in earnest. My shell was stuck to my down and I just could't get out! I heard a crack at the other end of my shell and my tail stuck out. There I was, trapped in my shell, with my tail out one end and my bill out the other! I was *ever so* tired. Again I rested -- perhaps a long time.

When I awakened, I could see out of my shell with one eye. It was quiet. It was v-e-r-y q-u-i-e-t. Where was my mother? I heard clucking off in the distance. My mother was leaving the nest with my brothers and sisters! She had forgotten me!

I had been struggling for a day while the other ducklings hatched and felt the warmth of real mother contact. They were leaving -- going down the dock. Mallard ducks never come back to the nest with their young. I peeped and peeped and peeped. "Mother, wait for me -- W-A-I-T!" It was too late -- she had to protect the other ducklings and get them some food and water.

It was too late. I was stuck in my shell -- crying. It was dark. I was alone, and I was SCARED!

Suddenly I was lifted up in the air. Warm hands were around me and my shell. I looked into Jane's eyes!

Holding me carefully, she hurried up the hill. She spoke gently to me in a language I didn't understand, yet I felt she wouldn't harm me. She was searching for Don. He met her half way up the path and together they discussed what to do for me.

I peeped, peeped and peeped! Would they help me escape from my trap? I wanted to be free and I was very thirsty! Their gentleness and their friendly chatter soothed me, and I was less afraid.

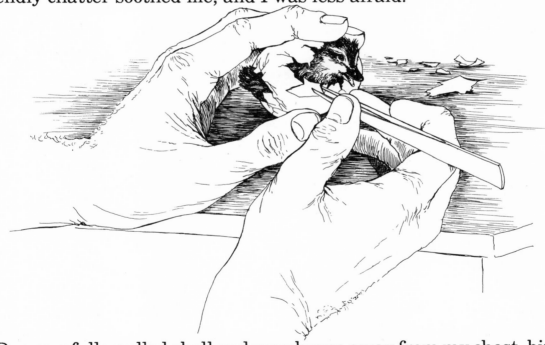

Don carefully pulled shell and membrane away from my chest, bit by bit with his tweezers. I wiggled to help. My head was completely free, my chest, then my legs. More and more shell pieces lay aside. "Peep, peep!" How wonderful! But large pieces of shell and membrane were still attached to the down on my wings. Don was struggling to remove more shell when he stopped and put down the tweezers. It pulled and really hurt. He was afraid of injuring me. I looked up at him gratefully. Our eyes met. Jane and Don were now my new mother and father.

My, but I was strong in spite of the shell still attached to my wings. They stood back to look at me. I hopped around the table, happy that I could stretch my legs. My legs supported me! I was still sticky -- but I was strong.

Don decided I was "Super Duck" because I was so eager to survive. I just wouldn't stop hopping, peeping, and jumping around. I even tried to flap my wings, but they were still stuck.

Perhaps because I had spent several days in my shell struggling while the other ducks hatched, I had grown strong. Don and Jane agreed that I was Super Duck, and I was Super Duck from that time on.

I tilted my head to get a better look at what they were doing. I lost my balance and fell over. I could't get my feet down. I couldn't use my wings to turn over because they were stuck to my sides. I twisted and kicked. I was determined to be on my feet! Jane helped turn me right side up. She rubbed my bill. It felt good.

Don put a little water in a glass baking dish and sprinkled bits of chick starter mash into it. Curiously, I peeked over the edge. I didn't know what to do.

He put his finger in the pan and held the moistened finger close to my bill. I opened my bill and sucked in some water. It was wonderful! I was so thirsty! I followed his finger into the pan and took my first real drink. In my eagerness water went into my nostrils and I sneezed. I soon got used to drinking properly. I would tip my bill upward, stretch my neck and the water would go down so much better.

Was I happy! I hopped into the pan and swizzled water and twittered, shaking with joy right down to my tail!

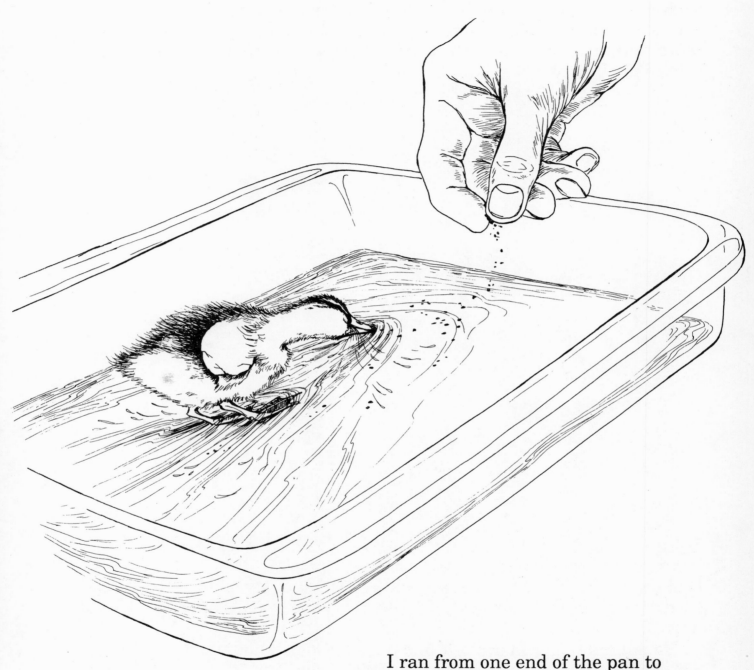

I ran from one end of the pan to
the other, splashing water with my feet
in my eagerness to drink. I ran my bill under
the water swizzling with pleasure. Then I began to
peck and suck in little specks of the mash. The specks
tasted very good so I continued to twitter, swizzle and peck
until I was completely full.

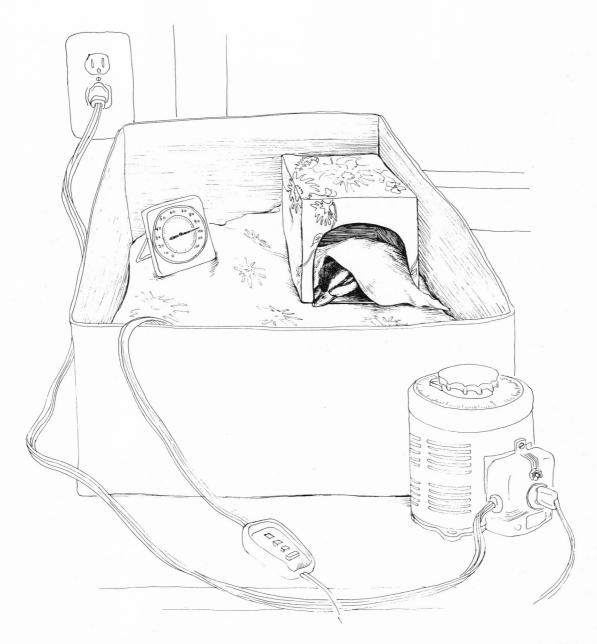

I now needed warmth. Don knew what to do. He put me in a small box with a heating pad, some cotton cloth and a thermometer. A tiny pan of water and mash was in the corner. My wings were getting very heavy, especially with the shell attached. I snuggled down into the warmth -- contented.

Don was busy adjusting the temperature of the heating pad until he was satisfied with a steady 95-degree reading on the thermometer. I closed my eyes, then opened them and gave a short happy twitter.

"Good night little Super Duck," they said and covered my box so it was cozy and dark. I gave a last quiet peep, peep and fell fast asleep.

For three days Jane sprayed water on my wings to soften the remaining shell. Each day Don was able to take more shell off with his tweezers. He was so gentle it didn't hurt at all. I was all wiggles, active and eager to explore the world around me.

You can imagine how happy I was to be finally free of my shell. Their worried looks turned to smiles when they realized my wings were not injured. Jane rubbed my bill and my chest. I was about the happiest duckling that ever lived!

Day and night blended into one another. I was especially happy when Don and Jane were around. If they left me too long I could be very demanding -- peeping and screeching.

My brothers and sisters led a much harder life. Dewy would often keep them moving up and down the hill. When they were at the feeding station they "tanked up" as Don would say. They didn't have food next to them all day long. When they did feed, their crops hung almost to the ground.

At night they had to hide in the shallow marsh grass and hope they weren't seen. I was always snug in my warm bed, indoors and protected. Dewy, ever alert, hovered over my brothers and sisters to protect them when a hawk flew over. She spread her wings to try to cover ten active ducklings. They would freeze, not moving at all until danger was gone.

No one had to teach me about Hawks!   I would freeze, too, even though I was protected by my wire outdoor cage. When a hawk went soaring high above, I knew!

There are many dangers for little ducklings, besides hawks. Snapping turtles, large fish, otters, foxes, and raccoons can make a fine meal out of ducklings like me! It pays to be always watchful!

It may seem strange, but my mother Dewy faded more and more from my mind. I forgot I ever was a duckling. In fact, I really thought I was a "people-person" like my adopted mother and father.

I was pretty contented and spoiled although I was grateful for the attention they gave me and very lonely when they weren't around.

One day when I was about four days old Don and Jane bought me a present -- my own Teddy Bear! He seemed so big, cuddly and friendly. I liked to work over his face, his ears, eyes, and nose. Then I would settle down for a nap between his soft legs, resting my bill on his tummy. He was wonderful company. Wherever I went, Jane and Don brought Teddy too.

The first few weeks I slept in the studio snug in my small cardboard container, with Teddy, food, water, and a little tissue box house. Don and Jane slept across the room. I would wake up much earlier than they did. For a while I would be happy to splash and swizzle my mash. Finally I wanted their companionship and would I squawk! -- "Peep, peep, peep, peep."

Jumping up on my little tissue box box house I tried as hard as I could to peek over the edge. I carried on so steadily, that finally in desperation, Jane came to fetch me. I knew she would! My peeps then changed to twitters on first sight of her.

She let me explore under the covers while she and Don had an extra few minutes of rest.

Mind you -- they didn't sleep! I wouldn't let them. I was a bundle of energy, actively nibbling at their toes, fingers, and finally their faces. Sternly Jane said, "Enough, Super Duck" and promptly got up.

With Teddy in one hand and me cuddled in her other arm, we headed for the kitchen.

What fun the kitchen was! In the nooks and crannies under the cabinets I found delicious spiders and bugs to eat. "Click-click, click; click-click,click" -- the rhythm of my toenails could be heard across the room as I raced from one spot to another.

The floor was especially slippery and I skidded and slithered, finding myself upside down. Either Don or Jane helped turn me over. Then I stretched my little wings "slap-flap" jumping on my toes, scurrying off for more pecking at bugs and things.

At first I couldn't hold my wings up for very long, even after the shell was removed. They drooped, especially when I was whining or crying.

My favorite pleasure was snuggling up to Don's or Jane's bare feet. I tickled their toes with my bill and then settled down on their feet to preen and sleep. Little trills of pleasure and soft twitters came from my throat during sleep.

I was a little ball of endless energy and I wanted to be with them all the time. What a fuss I made when they tried to sneak away! When I wanted to be held, I snuggled up to one of them and started pecking furiously.

I especially liked to disturb Don when he was reading. "Squawk, peep," I cried until he picked me up in his lap and stroked my bill. With a few happy shudders of my body, maybe a bit of feather preening and one eye cocked to look at him, I'd settle into a wonderful nap.

Before supper you could often find us in their solarium. We gathered for social chatter. The room was full of plants and had a thick white rug that I enjoyed nesting into for a snooze. Best of all were the fantastic spiders and bugs I found poking around the potted plants. Once, in my eagerness to catch a special bug, I knocked over a pot. Dirt spilled on the white carpet. I was spoken to very sternly. I tilted my head and looked up sadly -- straight into their eyes. All was forgiven.

I was constantly preening my down and Jane can tell you what a mess it made in the kitchen.

Large balls of fluff rolled under the table and chairs. For that reason I was finally banned from the rest of the house.

At first, I didn't have my oil gland developed but pretended it was there on my tail. Rubbing and nibbling with my bill I fixed all my "feathers" -- well -- they really weren't feathers exactly -- at least not yet.

I was growing. I could see my body changing and elongating with tail feathers appearing. I was about two and a half weeks old. Gradually tiny brown feathers started appearing on my chest and wings. Little by little my golden yellow and dark brown down-covered body was actually graying! The down created a halo of fuzz that I was continually removing along with bits and pieces of shaft.

It felt good, and I cooed and chirped while preening. It kept me very busy indeed. It kept Don and Jane busy, too, cleaning up after me. I remember Don said one time as he swept the fluff off the floor, "How could one little duck have *so* much fuzz!" It got worse, too, as I grew older!

y life was very exciting! I had a protected wire cage outdoors where I could enjoy the warm August sun. Don had fixed a garden hose to drip fresh water slowly into my cage. I loved to suck on the pipe before the water dropped down. It was my own drinking fountain! I buried my bill in the mud created by the dripping water and drilled holes and slurped up the mixture. What fun that was -- slurping up mud, bugs, and water!

My wonderful Teddy Bear sat beside my new wooden house. To tell you the truth, I didn't often sleep inside the house. I much preferred to sleep near Teddy or up on the roof. I felt lots taller there. It was a grand place to look for Jane and Don.

Oh, I almost forgot to tell you about my wonderful pool. It was really a rubber dish pan, but it suited me perfectly. When Jane first filled it with water to the top, I was puzzled.

I had never been for a real swim. Don and Jane were afraid I might drown. I wasn't water-proofed. I had never had oil rubbed on my down.

My brothers and sisters were buoyant from the first day. They had crawled in and out of Dewy's feathers. Her oil rubbed off, protecting them. They did all their swimming in the big river.

Well, I can tell you I didn't mind. I had the life! I surprised everyone, myself included. The edge of the pool was high and I was afraid to jump over, but Don put a stepping stone for me to use. I was a natural swimmer. I shoved off at one end, swimming underwater, holding my breath and circling the pan. What fun it was! I popped right up, splashing water everywhere and continued my underwater streaking until at last I was soaked completely. They were right.
I wasn't waterproof.

Hopping up on my wooden house, I began my preening in frantic earnest, starting on my chest and working back to my tail. Sucking in the water with my bill, I threw it off by shaking my bill back and forth. Tiny droplets of water went flying! It's ever so important to keep feathers clean and neat.

I loved to stretch my leg and wing. You would have laughed to see me attempt this acrobatic stunt at first. I tumbled a lot. I didn't have much wing for balance.

When I was about three weeks old they decided it was time for me to have my own sleeping area. I liked to go to bed at dusk, but I awakened early too. I was eager to get going in the morning. And I was noisy about it!.

Don put two huge cartons together, with a passway between. I had two rooms. One was my kitchen with food and water; the other was my bedroom with wonderful Teddy and blankets.

This two-room apartment was in Don's shop, right below the studio where they slept. I could *still* wake them up! You see, I had developed a loud "Quack!" It would carry great distances, and I wasn't afraid to use it to my advantage!

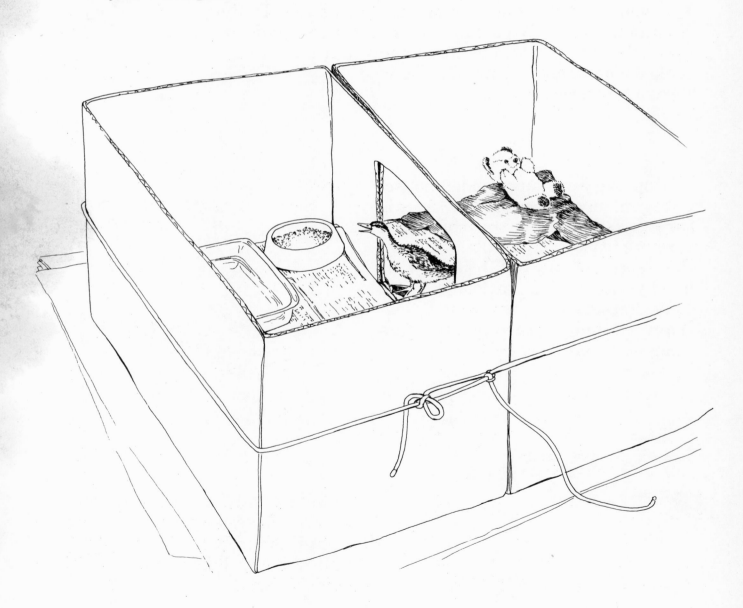

Of course, Jane would let me out. With much flapping of wings, with feathers and down flying, I hopped up and down. My morning exercises over, I followed Jane.

Everyday we went to pick up the newspaper at the gate. Sometimes I found a bug and became distracted. It tasted so good. I looked up and she would be far ahead. Squawking, I cried, "Wait for me!" She always smiled sweetly, "Well, hurry up Super Duck."

Once or twice Jane teased me and tried to hide. Did I set off a fuss! Hopping and running in circles I finally found her. Then I ran after her as fast as I could and tucked my bill under her arm, content.

    Soon after that
I was invited to my
very own party. My first
real party! Ginny and O. J.
were neighbor friends, and they wanted ME to visit. We walked down the
road -- a happy family. I bounced here and there looking for a bug, then
tried to catch up. I was very hot and my little legs grew tired. Jane carried
me part of the way, to my great relief.

    Ginny and O. J. had already placed a large pan of water on their terrace
just for me. It was refreshing to have a drink, but I didn't show off. I didn't
swim, even though Jane wanted me to demonstrate how good an underwater
swimmer I was. I just didn't, that's all! I was too happy having four sets
of feet to nibble at. They fussed over me. I twittered, bouncing and pecking
everywhere.

    It was a great party -- maybe because I was the star. That night I slept
so soundly Jane had to wake me in the morning. I don't remember if I
dreamed, but I was grateful for having such a wonderful home and family.
I loved Jane and Don a lot! Even when I was demanding!

One day I was resting
in my wire cage. I tipped my
head to listen. I was nervous!
The wind picked up and the sky
darkened. It rumbled off in the
distance. What was happening to
my world? The rumbling grew louder.
I was scared! I ran to Teddy Bear.
He was no help at all. I wanted Don
or Jane to come fast! Would they hear
my peeping? I threw myself around the cage
and jumped up on my house.

The rain started, slowly at first. Then
I felt the sky itself falling. How it rained!
I was one soaked, frightened duckling.
"Where were Don and Jane?" I shivered. I
tried to shake the water off, but I wasn't yet a
waterproof duck. "HELP!"

Then, there they were! Oh how happy I was! Don opened the wire
top and carried me, wet down, feathers and all, into the house. I can tell
you it took a lot of time to fix my feathers after *that* experience!

I had another unusual experience. Don and Jane decided to take me with them on a boat trip. The trip was to be an overnight anchoring in a cove of the Chesapeake Bay.

The whole experience was distressing! I didn't like the vibration of the motor. I was frightened and let them know it. With a mixture of peeps and quacks I frantically tried to keep one or the other next to me for the whole trip. Jane liked to ride "top-side" with Don who was navigating. I didn't like it.

I was in my wire cage with my swimming pool and Teddy nearby. The water was sloshing back and forth -- mostly on the deck. I certainly didn't want to swim. I felt sick! I wanted Jane.

She was disgusted with my constant quacking. I didn't care! I wanted Jane. Finally she put her foot over the side by the ladder and I was happy. I knew where she was at last. Oh how I loved her feet! Yes -- it was enough to keep me quiet, and I suspect she was happy too.

After the anchor had been placed I was free to explore the boat. I must say that was a lot better! The vibrations had stopped. Best of all, the flies had arrived! Don kept a fly swatter busy, and I kept the boat clean! As soon as I heard the splack of the swatter, I ran. I was Super Duck -- I knew -- flies were yum yum! I loved them next best to crickets. Splack went the swatter, and I would twitter, coo and shiver with joy. Another wonderful fly to digest.

The next day we returned home. It was my last boat trip. Thank goodness!!!

I must not forget to tell you about crickets. This was the "year of the cricket." Quite by accident I discovered they were my favorite food. When I was still very young I chased them across the room. Sometimes, at first, they would get away, but I soon learned how to snap them up! I couldn't eat a whole cricket in one gulp, as I did later on. My throat was too small, so I broke them up with my bill and ate all the pieces, including the legs!

Don began gathering crickets at night. He collected live crickets in a peanut butter jar with air holes.

All the while I was sleeping soundly in my apartment in the shop. I could hardly wait to get up in the morning. As soon as I saw that jar I twittered and shook my whole body. My bill even vibrated.

Don opened the jar, releasing his live evening catch -- usually three or four. I skittered and pounced -- gulp, gulp, gulp! -- as quick as one, two, three, they were all gone! Then I hurried to my water pan, took a few large slurps, held my head high and let the water trickle down my throat. It was a routine I never tired of. How I loved crickets!

When I was very little I spent a lot of time in my wire outdoor cage. Don was afraid a hawk might grab me. I was only free to run through grass and ivy and explore the big, big world when they were around. Just about everyday they had picnic lunches on the point. I enjoyed them, too. Don was a fast walker. I had to hurry to catch up. Sometimes in my haste I almost tripped his feet. I wouldn't let him out of my sight.

I picked up large acorns and tried to eat them. Of course, they were too large for me to eat, but I pecked at them anyway. I often found an ant run and slurped up numbers of delicious ants. But most of all I just wanted to be near Don and Jane -- to snuggle content at their feet, or sleep in a lap with my bill buried under my wing.

ater, when I was six weeks old, Don built an open shelter for me. I was free outdoors all the time. I now know what they were trying to do, but at that time I was confused.

I really didn't like being free and hopped up the brick steps to the back door stoop to quack and quack and quack! They couldn't fool me! I could see them peeking from behind the bedroom curtains.

They wanted me to be more independent. They wanted me to become a duck now that I had many of my juvenile feathers. But they knew it would take time for me to get used to being on my own, so they started early.

That's *not* what I wanted. I wanted THEM!! If I kept quacking long enough someone would surely come and comfort me. I still had my Teddy, my swimming pool, and my water hose under my new open shelter. My wire cage had been put away.

It felt strange. I didn't like the idea at all. I spent a lot of time on the back stoop and going to the shop door too -- back and forth -- until I was tired. That's when I welcomed the shade under the shelter, or the pool. I almost filled up the pool now, I had grown so big. I couldn't swim in it anymore, but I could dunk and bathe. It's funny, but Teddy kept looking smaller and smaller all the time. In fact, I was much bigger than Teddy, but I still loved him and still cuddled with my bill on his leg.

As my body grew, my legs became stronger. I was developing some very handsome feathers. On the sides of my wings a beautiful blue patch appeared with thin white stripes on each side. This was my flashy speculum. It grew quickly. At first it was only a half inch patch of blue, but finally was four inches wide. When I stretched my wing its length was much, much longer. I loved to run my bill over it. Now I had a real wing and I would tuck my bill under it when I slept. It was heavenly.

My primary feathers were beginning to develop, too. They would eventually be my flying feathers, but now they looked strange -- like little paddles on the end of sticks, ten funny sticks all lined up. Everyday they grew. I preened them just right. Running my bill through the feathers, smoothing them, I took out bits and pieces of down and shaft.

My white underfeathers were growing at the same time and becoming quite thick. They helped keep me warm all the time. I was getting respectable wings to flap, and what a noise they made!

Each morning, I stretched my wings, flapping them just as I had done every day since I was born. Now they almost supported me. I wanted to fly! I wasn't ready -- not yet, anyway, but I tried. My breast muscles were getting stronger, too.

Jane and Don still allowed me in the kitchen, even though the puffs of down I left behind were awful. I slept at their feet during meals, but I spent more and more time outside. They encouraged me to eat at the feeding station for the other ducks. Other ducks? Was I really a duck? Except -- "(You want to know a s-e-c-r-e-t?" "Quack" -- I wanted to fly)!

Don had placed my shelter near their walkway. I think he hoped we'd all get acquainted. HA! I watched with detachment as the various ducks crowded around the corn and water. Sometimes they fought and pecked and shoved to get at the food.

Personally, I thought they were silly. I stood under my shelter, separate. Was I really like them? I didn't think so. No, I didn't think so at all, not until much later.

After eating all the corn they wanted they started to chatter. They jibbered and jabbered, discussing whether to walk or fly back to the waterfront. Suddenly with a s-w-o-o-s-h, those ducks that could fly lifted straight up in the air and maneuvered easily through the pines, landing gracefully on the river.

The young ducks that couldn't fly waddled quickly down the path. There they joined the others, splashing and quacking, glad to find their families again.

Did you know even the adult ducks can't fly for about a month while they are molting? They lose all their primary feathers. Their new feathers start growing immediately. It happens every year, late in the summer.

The handsome drakes (male ducks) lose all their brilliant color. Now they look a lot like the molting hens (female ducks). Sometimes the drakes look downright funny with patches of green blotched with brown on their heads and necks. Their black and gray bodies become totally eclipsed into mottled browns. Their iridescent green heads and white neck rings disappear too. Only their blue speculum remains the same.

This is a dangerous time for them. They have to hide on the water, away from their enemies. It is amazing how they are somewhat camouflaged and protected by their eclipse plumage.

Ducks feel water is the safest place to be. You seldom see ducks facing away from the water when they're sleeping. Not smart ducks! By the time they can fly again most of the young ducks can fly, too. Isn't it wonderful that it all happens at about the same time?

Three or four times a day Don or Jane walked me over to the food dishes. I never went there by myself. There was mash in one pan and whole corn in several others. I began to like corn. Now that I could eat a cricket in one gulp, I could swallow whole corn, too.

After filling my crop, I walked down the path to the river with Don and Jane. They were trying to set a pattern for me similar to the other ducks. The river looked enormous! I couldn't see across.

By late summer in Virginia the Bay waters are warm and full of life. Crabs were shedding their shells near the shore. A blue heron on great long legs was stalking and gobbling up as many soft crabs as he could find. I wasn't afraid of the heron even though he was huge. I felt he wouldn't hurt me.

Jane was coaxing me into the water. I was still afraid. There she was up to her knees in the river. "Come on Super Duck, come to me. You will like the water," Jane pleaded. Holding her skirt up to keep it dry, she continued gently calling me.

I didn't like all the THINGS in the water. It was salty, too! I especially didn't like the waves. They reminded me of that dreadful boat trip, maybe worse. They seemed to attack me repeatedly, without letting up!

With encouragement from Jane, I moved closer to her. Suddenly I was over my head! I floated beautifully! My feathers were well oiled now from my own oil gland. Every time I preened I rubbed oil over my feathers.

I let the waves lift and lower me. I became less afraid. I rubbed her legs and was happy. Where were her feet? Hey -- this was fun! Where were her feet? I dove. There they were! Happily, I swam around under water, popping up, then repeating the underwater ballet. Round and round, in and out I went, occasionally giving her feet a nip with my bill.

Instinctively, I pulled my primary feathers into my developing wing pockets to keep them dry. This would be important later when I wanted to use them for flying. Feathers are designed to trap air, but if they get wet or disorderly there is trouble -- real trouble! It also made me streamlined, gliding smoothly under the water. Plop! I was back on the surface. Jane was smiling. I was happy too. I flapped my wings and took a splashing bath.

We did this every day, sometimes several times a day, from then on. We even did it when the water got colder in the fall. It wasn't always a long swim if the "no see 'ems" (gnats) decided to swarm on Jane at dusk. They didn't bother me, but Jane didn't like them. So we would hurry up the path.

Often the other ducks would come over to look at me. That's when I swam as fast as I could to the protection of Jane's legs. She spent hours on her lawn chair, reading or sketching, with her feet dangling over the edge of the sand. She hoped I would go in the water without her, but, no, I would not! I stayed next to her feet. Well -- almost -- sometimes I drilled little holes in the sand and found new flavored things to eat. I stretched, preened and slept, but I never went into the water without her -- never!

Several groups of ducks lazily explored the shore line. I watched and saw ducks working the sand under the water with their strong legs and feet. They made sand and mud clouds. "Tipping up" they searched the disturbed sand for interesting things to eat. Often they found snails, worms, and shrimp and parts of water plants. Their tails were up and their heads were down. I looked around for Jane. She told me they were dabbling ducks and that I was a dabbling duck, too. I didn't believe her then.

There were mallard ducks everywhere on the waterfront. In the warmth of the Virginia sun most were sleeping. They lined up facing the water in little family groups. Some were sleeping in the shade of the canoe. Occasionally, they would "nudge" other ducks' tails, to move them and take their places. Don called it "musical chairs."

Usually one or two ducks would be on the alert. The rest would stretch, preen, and often sleep.

Fixing feathers is about the most important thing a duck can do. It's something like combing your hair, but all the feathers must be clean and straight. It's a long stretch of the neck to reach all the feathers. Sometimes you can shake your body and all the feathers fall in place. That's also when a lot of old feathers go flying! Some end up floating on the surface of the water.

I watched as one duck hesitated when he lifted his leg. He extended it and shook off some sand. When he returned it under his feathers he was fast asleep, balancing on one leg. I like to do that, too.

Ducks really enjoy fresh water. Perhaps that's why they spend so much time near the water tub in Don's and Jane's yard. In the summer the river becomes very salty.

During a rainfall the ducks got very excited over the runoff from the boathouse. I saw them fight over the drain down spout "drinking fountain." They pushed each other away so they could tilt their heads and collect the fresh water, before it mixed into the river water. I had my own water fountain up the path under my shelter.

The ducks enjoyed nibbling at the dock piles. All ducks enjoy eating the many tasty and nourishing things attached to the piles.

I just watched and learned.

his was a happy time. I kept growing. There was a crispness in the air, as the days became shorter. September was moving quickly towards October. Our daily routines continued. I came in at night, glad to rest securely after a busy day.

One day, Elizabeth arrived. She came for a visit. Don and Jane were happy. Elizabeth was one of their children. I was happy too. She gave me lots and lots of attention. She liked watching me swim.

We spent a lot of time around the waterfront. The three of them chatted and caught up on the latest news. They sat near the water on lawn chairs. I sat underneath, watching them, or pecking and swizzling in the sand. Sometimes -- sometimes I enjoyed pecking at their legs or bottoms that were exposed between the webbing of the chairs. I couldn't understand why they didn't like it.

One day they decided to take a trip on that awful boat. I could tell, because they spent so much time going out on the dock carrying things. I followed, but I didn't like the dock at all. I didn't like that BIG boat either.

I watched from shore. I set up a terrible fuss quacking, then decided to swim out to the boat. I had never been out that far before. In fact I had never been in the water before without either Don or Jane. "Quaack-quaack!" I screeched, shaking all over and working my little legs as fast as I could.

Suddenly one leg was caught! I was being pulled under the water. What was happening? "Help," I squawked. "Help me!" I fought and fought, making quite a splash in the water, thrashing frantically to stay above the surface.

With super strength I kicked loose, only to see a blue crab scurrying sideways away from me. I was free! Who did he think he was anyway? I was much too big for him to eat and much too strong.

My leg hurt for sometime afterwards where he held me with his claw. I was much more careful after that experience. I guess everything one does is a part of learning, but it certainly is difficult to grow up. That's exactly what I was doing.

I swam back to the protection of the shore, quickly! Jane and Elizabeth came to comfort me. When they realized I was fine they left to take their ride on the boat. I was a very sad duck. I was alone. I'm sure they could hear me squawking even when they rounded the point. Then I went up the path to my Teddy Bear, snuggled down and went to sleep.

It wasn't long before I heard the motor of the boat again. They were home, and what a reunion we had! I twittered and shook my tail and flapped my wings. I practically jumped into their arms.

One day I did the unthinkable! Something I never thought I would do. I went down the path to the river -- alone! It suddenly felt safe and friendly.

I didn't need Don and Jane's company as much anymore.

I was becoming a duck. I had strange urges.

I still enjoyed the kitchen. I still enjoyed going for the morning paper with Jane. I still hopped up on the back stoop and squawked when I wanted inside and ran straight to my water dish. And of course I still loved the crickets Don gave me every morning. Oh yes, my apartment was comforting at night with Teddy next to me, too.

I was almost completely developed. I only had a little down left on my head and neck. The rest of me was thick with insulating feathers. It wouldn't be long now before I would be flying. I practiced, getting better every day.

Then strange events took place which changed my life forever. There was a lot of attention being given my apartment and outdoor shelter. Neighbors came and were given a "tour" of my routine. SOMETHING WASN'T RIGHT. I met Georgia and Kay and Ken. They talked and talked with Don and Jane. It was confusing. I didn't understand.

Then they were gone. Don, Jane, and Elizabeth were gone! I think they tried to tell me they were leaving for a visit to New England. They were ever so loving to me that night and kept me way past my bedtime.

As they carried suitcases to the car the next morning, I kept up a constant quacking. I pecked at their shoes and untied Don's shoelaces. I made a real nuisance of myself. Elizabeth tried to distract me by going around the house twice. "Quack, quack, quack!" They had driven away! Don and Jane had left me! They were gone for a week -- but I didn't know that at the time.

That first day, I was very lonely. Where had my family gone? I couldn't understand. I spent all of the day under my shelter sulking and on the back door stoop. No one opened the door to let me in.

Finally, dejected and heartbroken, I headed for the friendly river. There with the flock of mallard ducks as company, I floated, dabbled tail up, swam and snoozed under the late September warmth.

The sun began to slip below the western shore and the glow of lavender, pink, and orange reflected on the rippling river. The first long, long day was almost over. I wasn't quite so sad. I enjoyed being near the other ducks.

I usually sat and swam apart from them, but I listened to their constant conversation. They didn't seem quite so silly now.

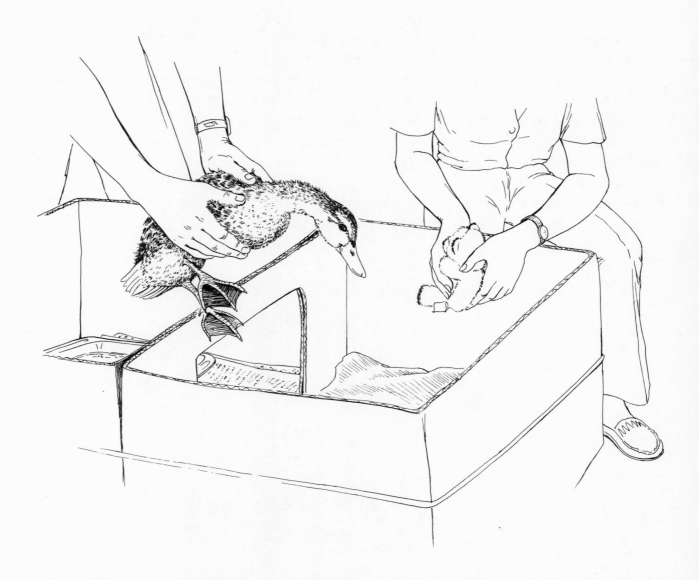

I heard my name called -- "Super Duck, Super Duck." It didn't sound like Don's voice. But it *was* my name and I *was* being called. I waddled up the path and met Kay and Ken with a jar full of crickets!

I tipped my head to get a better look at them. Kay told me to call them "Aunt" and "Uncle." I remembered, they were friends of Don and Jane. They had been looking at my apartment the day before.

With a happy twitter and shake of my tail I promptly swallowed four or five crickets. They tasted so good. Aunt Kay and Uncle Ken became my friends. Uncle Ken lifted me up and gently carried me to bed. My apartment looked wonderful and safe. Aunt Kay placed Teddy next to my clean blankets and gave me fresh corn and water. I twittered, gave a soft quack, closed my eyes and was asleep before they closed the shop door.

When morning came Georgia opened the door, lifted me out of my apartment and let me outdoors. I gave her a happy, grateful quack. She changed the water in my pool and added fresh water to the round tub the other ducks used. She filled up the food dishes with corn. (I no longer required starter mash). She then placed Teddy under my shelter and told me to have a good day.

She didn't fool me! She wasn't going to stay. I wanted "people" company. I waddled right up to her front door.

"Quack, quaack," I fussed loudly. She wouldn't let me in. Reluctantly, I went back to my shelter and Teddy Bear.

Some mornings she tried to hide and slip quietly away. I would have none of that! She ducked behind bushes, but I always caught up with her on the other side. Georgia wouldn't have any of that either and told me so in no uncertain terms. "Now Super Duck, you stay home!" she exclaimed. But she had affection in her voice. I hesitated, looked at her sadly -- hesitated --and - then returned to my shelter.

My routine really hadn't changed that much since Don and Jane left - - except that I didn't have their kitchen to enjoy. I thought of Georgia as another Aunt. Aunt Kay, Uncle Ken, and Aunt Georgia became my friends.

Now I was more adventuresome and swam with the flock around our point of land. Still, I was timid, and stayed a little behind the others. I swam farther than I ever had before. I might have kept on going when I heard Uncle Ken's voice calling me.

What should I do? I did want to find out where the other ducks were headed, but it was growing dark, and I knew Uncle Ken had crickets. The crickets won out. That night they gave me extra attention and extra crickets.

Generally, there is harmony among the waterfront creatures, but sometimes there are territorial disputes. All of a sudden there was such a racket! The osprey and the great blue heron were attacking each other in mid-air.

The osprey had a nest off our point. The young were quite capable by this time of year, but spoiled. Papa and Mama Osprey still brought them fish even though they could fly. The young stood on their nesting pole and screeched for food.

I suspect that Papa Osprey was still trying to protect his fledglings. The heron was distracted, looking for fish and crabs to eat and had made the mistake of flying too close. Both are huge birds, but the heron is truly the biggest. His wing spread is almost seven feet. The osprey with his six foot wing span and sharp talons can be more dangerous.

With a frenzied shrill "Chewk, chewk, cheereek" the osprey attacked.

The herons response was frightening, harsh sounds. "Awak, awak, awak!"

Their shadows briefly loomed over me. Then they moved on, continuing their fight over the boathouse. "Awak, awak" -- Cheereek!"

Their battle was over almost as suddenly as it began. The osprey, still in a fury, returned to his nesting pole and family. The heron flew west over the river. No one was the winner. I was glad when it was over. I did *not* like their noises!

he week went more quickly than I could imagine. Don and Jane had returned! There was much fussing, hugging, and stroking my bill and chest.

I was in the kitchen at last -- that wonderful kitchen -- and I was eagerly nibbling and pecking at their shoes and stockings. I cocked my head and looked and looked. Yes, there they were! My family, together again. I settled down in Don's lap and tucked my head and bill under his arm.

But I was different. Somehow I was really different. I spent more and more time every day away from Don and Jane, away with the other ducks. I really knew who I was now, a duck, a mallard duck -- well maybe Super Duck, too! Something special was about to happen.

One day it happened. I was ready for the big event -- my solo flight! No one had to tell me I was ready or how to fly. I knew.

When you take off in flight you lift up into the wind, and I can tell you, it would take forever if you tried any other way, especially if there was any kind of breeze.

The wind helped me up, up and up. I could make it, I could, I could! I pulled my feet under me closely and the most wonderful feeling came over me. The wind lifted me higher and higher. I worked hard, flapping my wings constantly. The wind rushed by as I went higher still. Oh what fun!

There was more water than I had ever imagined. Water everywhere, fingers of rivers stretching into the great bay. Best of all were the marshlands. There were lots and lots of salt marshes. The marshes feed the bay with life and give protection to me, other ducks, and many wild birds.

I'm glad the marshes on our river haven't been destroyed. I could see the pines and oaks, the house, studio, boathouse, and boat.

There was our own marshland jutting out from the point where I had so many wonderful picnics. It jutted out right next to the osprey's nesting pole. The nest was empty. This was October and the osprey had headed south for the winter.

I banked and turned around over the boathouse, looked down at the water, and came back into the wind for a landing. With my legs spread wide and wings forward, I was down. I landed with a splash on the river near all the other ducks. It was enough for my first flight.

Don and Jane weren't there to see me, but I would show them soon.

All I could think about now was flying. The other young ducks were happy too. Little by little everyone had learned. All the ducks had their new primary feathers and were right up there soaring, turning sharply, lifting higher, wings beating rhythmically.

It was terribly hard for me to leave the other ducks. Don and Jane had to come looking for me at dusk. I was very busy and would forget to see the shadows lengthening. I really didn't want to go to bed. Well -- I wasn't sure how I felt. I wanted to follow the other ducks around the point. I was confused. I loved Don and Jane and my apartment, too!

It became harder and harder to answer Don's calls. One evening they looked and looked for me. They finally found me swimming in front of their land, way around their point of marsh grass. I was far away from our familiar cove and boathouse.

"Super Duck, Super Duckie," they called. I hesitated just as I had when Uncle Ken had called me about a week before. Then I peeled off from the other ducks.

Quacking loudly -- "I'm coming -- I'm coming," I climbed over huge rocks and waddled to Don and Jane. I was picked up, hugged, and put to bed.

The first night I didn't come home to sleep I was exhausted. I didn't rest much floating on the water. It was scary hearing all those night sounds in the rustling marshes. I was protected only by the number of ducks around me. They would have to teach me what to listen for.

Several days later I waddled up the walk to the familiar back stoop. Everything was the same. There was Teddy. Dear Teddy -- I really didn't need him anymore, but I sat down next to him anyway.

Then Jane
opened the
kitchen door.
I rushed in and
all the old memories
flooded back. They were
so happy to see me. "Oh what
a handsome Super Quacky Duck,"
Don said. I didn't want to be picked up and get my feathers disturbed. I twittered and collapsed at their feet and slept.

I woke up when Jane got up to do the breakfast dishes. I wanted to go out again and quacked!

Don understood, opened the door and said, "Good-bye little Super Duck -- you are free now -- you can make it!"

EPILOGUE

I can fly and I'm free. I have been accepted into the flock. It's February, and I'm six months old. My story took place during my first three months.

I recently attracted a handsome drake. Have you guessed by now -- I'm a hen, a female mallard?

Don first realized this fact when I started to quack in earnest, quite loudly! And does my voice carry! Drakes have a softer voice and they do a lot of mumbling -- at least I think so!

Well, this particular drake is a showoff, but I do like his attention to me. It's very thrilling when he displays in front of me, whistling. He thrusts his head in the water, then throws it back, scattering droplets everywhere, then whistles and grunts.

He's a showoff all right, flapping his wings on the surface of the water to get my attention. I like it a lot. We bobbed our heads up and down facing each other. I like that too.

Perhaps I will choose him for my "bond partner." I'm still so very young, but someday we might have our own family. Then I will take my ducklings up the hill to show to Don and Jane.